THE LEARNING WORKS SCIENCE

DINOSAURS

Written and Illustrated by Beverly Armstrong

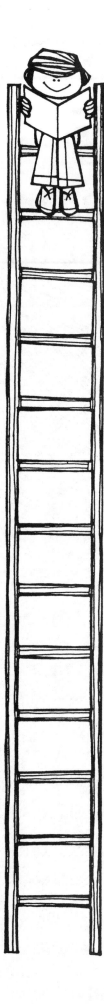

The Learning Works

Edited by Sherri M. Butterfield

Copyright © 1988
The Learning Works, Inc.
Santa Barbara, California 93160
All rights reserved.
Printed in the United States of America.

Contents

Allosaurus

This huge meat-eating dinosaur probably had no enemies once it reached adult size. Its thirty-five-foot body may have weighed four tons. The yard-long head had a gaping mouth lined with teeth like knife blades. Allosaurus could tear off and swallow huge chunks of meat from the animals that it killed. Apatosaurus and Stegosaurus frequently fell victim to this fast-moving predator. Allosaurus lived in the western United States and in Canada during the Jurassic period, more than 130 million years ago. Surprisingly, this great reptile's name does not describe its appearance or its behavior, but simply means "other lizard."

Activity Safari

1. We have no way of knowing what color the dinosaurs were. Some of today's reptiles, such as coral snakes, are brightly colored, while others, such as alligators, have dull, protective coloration. Some are mottled, or marked with stripes or spots. How do you think Allosaurus looked? Use words, paints, or pens to create a description of this dinosaur.

2. Many of the dinosaurs were very large, but there is an animal alive today that is bigger than any known dinosaur. It is almost three times as long as Allosaurus and may weigh more than thirty times as much. In Morse code, its name is

$$ \_ \cdot \cdot \cdot / \cdot \_ \cdot \cdot / \cdot \cdot \_ / \cdot / / \cdot \_ \_ / \cdot \cdot \cdot \cdot / \cdot \_ / \cdot \_ \cdot \cdot / \cdot $$

What animal is it? (If you are unfamiliar with Morse code, you can find it pictured and "decoded" in a dictionary or an encyclopedia.)

Allosaurus

Anatosaurus

Anatosaurus means "duck lizard," and this animal is sometimes called the duck-billed dinosaur. It lived in what are now the states of Wyoming and Montana and the Canadian province of Alberta during the Cretaceous period. A good swimmer, Anatosaurus spent much time in lakes and rivers, where it was protected from predators. This herbivore grazed on shrubs and used its specialized snout to gather underwater roots, leaves, and bulbs. These were ground to a pulp by the hundreds of teeth lining this dinosaur's jaws. Many well-preserved specimens of Anatosaurus have been found "mummified" in the lake beds where they died.

Activity Safari

1. An average adult Anatosaurus was fourteen feet tall. Make a bar graph on which you compare this size with the heights of at least five other dinosaurs. You may want to include your own height on the graph.

2. Design an amusement park with a dinosaur theme. Include rides, game booths, and refreshment stands. Name your park and draw a logo for it. You may wish to design a souvenir bumper sticker, T-shirt, or tote bag as well.

Anatosaurus

Ankylosaurus

This dinosaur's name means "stiffened lizard" or "fused lizard," and its body was certainly made rigid by the many plates of bone in its tough skin. Spikes protected its head and sides, and its tail was a massive bony club that could be swung to smash another animal's head or leg. All this armor effectively protected a slow-moving herbivore with blunt teeth and weak jaws. Ankylosaurus lived in western North America during the Late Cretaceous period, sharing its habitat with Anatosaurus, Triceratops, and Tyrannosaurus.

Activity Safari

1. Various sources report the length of this dinosaur as having been fifteen feet, seventeen feet, around twenty-five feet, more than thirty-two feet, and thirty-five feet. For what reason(s) might scientists have such different ideas about the length of Ankylosaurus?

2. Many "armored" animals walk the earth today. Learn about two or more of the animals listed below and compare the ways in which their "armor" protects them.

alligator	garden snail	lobster
armadillo	Goliath beetle	pangolin
box turtle	hedgehog	sea urchin

Ankylosaurus

Apatosaurus

Apatosaurus, the "deceptive lizard," is also known as Brontosaurus, or "thunder lizard." This seventy-foot-long, thirty-ton animal strolled the swamps and plains of Colorado, Oklahoma, Utah, and Wyoming during the Late Jurassic period. These slow-moving giants may have lived in herds like elephants. They browsed on tall trees, gathering food that other animals could not reach. Though their brains were small — about the size of a large apple — they probably had well-developed sight and hearing. If threatened, Apatosaurus could defend itself by lashing out with its long tail or hide by sliding into a deep lake and breathing through the nostril on top of its head.

Activity Safari

1. Tie several pieces of string together to make one piece seventy feet long. Grasp one end of the string and let a friend hold the other so that you are able to pull the string taut. Compare the length of your "Apatosaurustring" with the length of various buildings, fences, vehicles, and/or walls.

2. Although we can learn much about a dinosaur's appearance by studying its skeleton, there are many things we cannot find out in this way. For example, a rabbit's long ears do not "show up" on its skeleton, and elephant trunks and camel humps are also "invisible" if we look only at bones. Draw a picture of an Apatosaurus with some interesting nonbony body parts.

Apatosaurus

Brachiosaurus

The largest of all known dinosaurs, Brachiosaurus was about eighty feet long and may have weighed more than eighty tons. It was twenty feet tall at the shoulder and could swing its small head up to forty feet in the air. This animal was far more massive than Apatosaurus and had proportionately longer front legs. It gathered plant food, which was chewed with weak jaws before being passed along to the animal's huge stomach. Stones caught in the roots of torn-up shrubs and grasses were swallowed and may have helped Brachiosaurus grind and digest its food.

Activity Safari

1. The stones that were swallowed by dinosaurs are called **gastroliths.** This English word comes from two Greek words: **gaster,** meaning "stomach," and **lithos,** meaning "stone." Look up the words **gastro**pod and **mono**lith to find out what they mean.

2. Brachiosaurus weighed eighty tons. What combination of the animals listed below would equal that weight? You will need to use multiples of some animals. Many combinations are possible.

1 ton	bison	3 tons	rhinoceros
1½ tons	giraffe	4 tons	pilot whale
2 tons	walrus	7 tons	killer whale
2½ tons	hippopotamus	8 tons	elephant

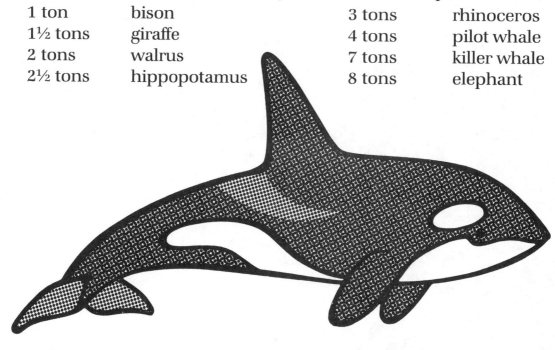

Brachiosaurus

Chasmosaurus

The "chasm" in this dinosaur's name refers to the large, skin-covered holes in its long, bony frill. These holes reduced the weight of the frill, but the animal still needed a strong neck to support its massive, three-horned skull. Chasmosaurus was about seventeen feet long and lived during the Late Cretaceous period. Skeletons of these animals have been found in the Canadian province of Alberta and in New Mexico. Tyrannosaurus shared Chasmosaurus's Canadian habitat and, doubtless, preyed on this herbivore.

Activity Safari

1. Make a word search using at least ten of these words.

Alberta	dinosaur	neck
bony	frill	prey
Canada	hole	skeleton
Chasmosaurus	horns	skull
Cretaceous	long	three

2. Several countries have printed stamps with dinosaurs on them. Design a stamp featuring your favorite prehistoric animal. Remember that a stamp must be labeled with its price and the name of the country issuing it.

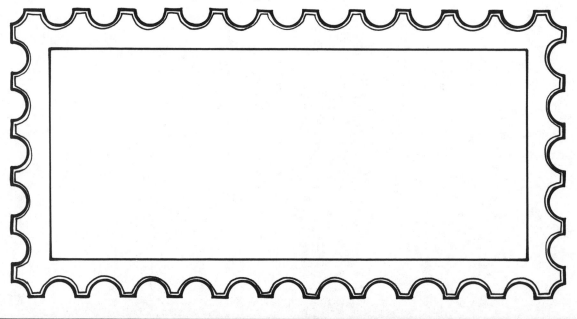

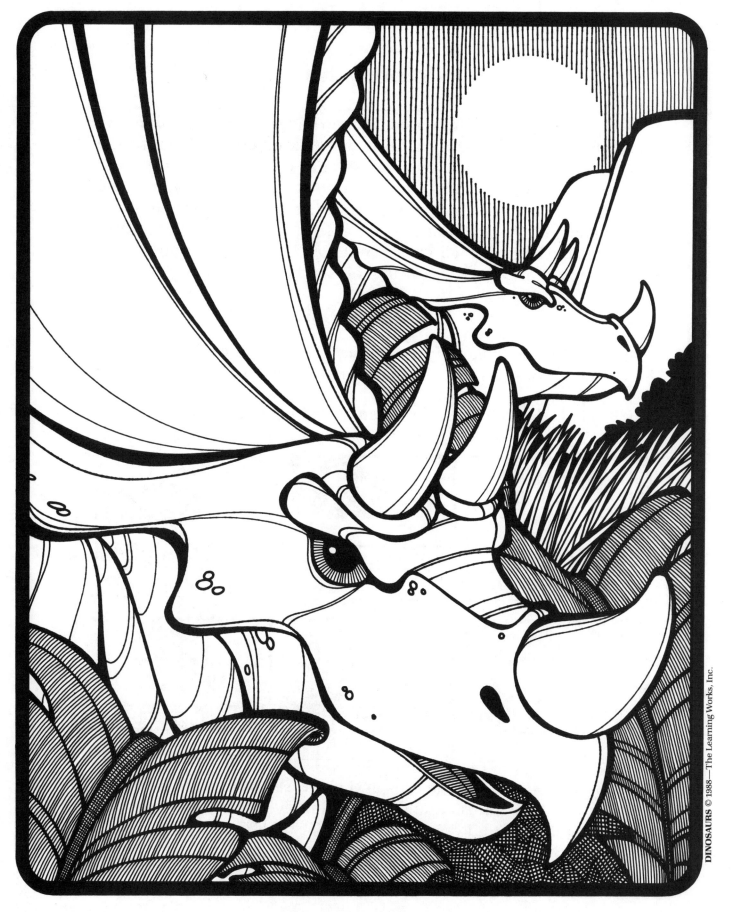

Chasmosaurus

Deinonychus

This agile, aggressive dinosaur is named for the "terrible claw" found on each of its hind feet — a huge, curved weapon that could slash with deadly force. Deinonychus's slender body was balanced by a long, rigid tail. Though only about five feet tall, this carnivore could easily catch and kill animals larger than itself by running them down and grabbing them with its strong, clawed front feet. Deinonychus had a large brain, good eyesight, and excellent coordination. It lived in western North America during the Early Cretaceous period.

Activity Safari

1. Use this code to identify the animals to which the pictured claws belong. Write the name of each animal on the line below its picture.

A B D E G H I K L M N O R S T

a. _____

b. _____

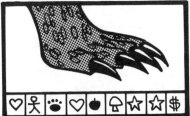

c. _____

d. _____

e. _____

f. _____

2. Deinonychus had large eyes and could see well. Many of today's reptiles have unusual and interesting eyes. Find and compare pictures of reptile eyes. Some especially weird ones are those of the geckos, chameleons, and snapping turtles.

Deinonychus

Iguanodon

One hundred and seventy years ago, no one knew that dinosaurs had ever existed. Iguanodon was the first one to be discovered. A tooth belonging to this prehistoric reptile was found in England in 1822. Later, the rest of that animal's skeleton was dug up and re-assembled. Since then, Iguanodons have been found in many parts of the world, including Africa, Asia, Europe, and North America. This animal was about fifteen feet tall, and its weight is estimated to have been between three and seven tons. Iguanodon had strong hind legs, a beak-like mouth, and strange spiked "thumbs." Living during the Cretaceous period, Iguanodon may have descended from the earlier Camptosaurus.

Activity Safari

1. Roll a four-inch square of paper into a cone and tape it over your thumb. In what ways does this spike hinder your hand's function? In what ways is it helpful? Think of and list some ways in which the Iguanodon might have used its thumb spikes.

2. Many lizards living today look like miniature dinosaurs. Just for fun, draw one of the lizards listed below in a city scene, where it is taller than the buildings.

   marine iguana   sungazer
   moloch   three-horned chameleon
   plumed basilisk   tokay gecko

Iguanodon

Lambeosaurus

Lambeosaurus lived near lakes and rivers in Late Cretaceous times. This odd-looking, fifty-foot-long dinosaur browsed on plants with its broad beak. Lambeosaurus had a hollow crest atop its head. In some specimens, this crest has been larger than the skull to which it is attached. These distinctive crests may have helped lambeosaurs recognize others of their own kind. Hollow tubes ran from the animal's nostrils to the crest cavity, so it is also possible that these strange structures enabled lambeosaurs to make hornlike sounds.

Activity Safari

1. Lambeosaurus was named after Lawrence Lambe, a Canadian paleontologist. If a dinosaur were named after you, what might it be called?

2. Try making growling, honking, and squealing sounds into various kinds of empty containers, such as a metal bucket or large can, a hose or cardboard tube, a plastic jug, and a paper cup. How do the sizes and shapes of these containers and the materials from which they are made affect the sounds? What might Lambeosaurus have sounded like?

Lambeosaurus

Spinosaurus

Spinosaurus, the "spiny lizard," lived in Africa during the Late Cretaceous period. The forty-foot-long animal may have weighed as much as seven tons. Its sharp, serrated teeth indicate that it was a carnivore. The most unusual feature of this dinosaur was a row of long spines that extended upward from its vertebrae, along its back. Some of these spines were more than six feet long, and it is likely that they supported a sail-like flap of skin.

This skin flap may have helped Spinosaurus adapt to the hot climate in which it lived by cooling the animal in much the same way that a radiator cools an automobile engine. Blood in vessels lying just beneath the relatively thin skin on this flap may have been cooled by exposure to breezes and moisture. This cooled blood could then have been circulated throughout the animal's body to help cool the rest of the beast.

Activity Safari

1. The sail of Spinosaurus may have kept this animal from fatally overheating. Some of today's desert animals have long, thin ears to help cool their bodies, while their cold-climate relatives have short, thick ears that are less susceptible to frostbite. Find and compare pictures of the Arctic fox and the fennec (a desert fox), or the snowshoe rabbit (also known as the varying hare) and the jackrabbit.

2. Spinosaurus looked a lot like Dimetrodon, a "mammal-like reptile" that lived *before* the dinosaurs. If a Dimetrodon hatched 250 million years ago and you had a penny for every year since its "birth," how many dollars would you have?

Spinosaurus

Stegosaurus

One of the best-known dinosaurs, Stegosaurus lived in western North America during the Late Jurassic period. The "plated lizard" was up to thirty feet long, weighed more than two tons, and had a brain smaller than a chicken egg. Along this dinosaur's back stood a series of bony plates, the largest of which was more than two feet long. The purpose of these plates is not known, but they probably helped to protect the animal in some way. Additional defense was provided by the powerful tail, which was armed with yard-long spikes. Allosaurus, Apatosaurus, and Brachiosaurus shared Stegosaurus's environment.

Activity Safari

1. If a Stegosaurus brain weighed two ounces and a human brain weighs three pounds, how many Stegosaurus brains would it take to equal the weight of one human brain?

2. Make a Stegosaurus hat. Enlarge the pattern below to 2-inch squares. Cut two dinosaur-shaped pieces from two 12-by-18-inch sheets of construction paper. Staple the pieces together as shown. You may want to fold the plates away from each other.

Stegosaurus

Struthiomimus

The seven-foot-tall "ostrich mimic" had a small head, a long neck, and strong legs. A long tail helped this animal keep its balance. Like an ostrich, Struthiomimus could run fast and kick with great force. Its front legs could be used for either digging or grasping. Struthiomimus probably ate a varied diet that included soft plants and fruit, eggs, insects, and small reptiles and mammals. Its beak was toothless but could be used for tearing food into small pieces. This dinosaur apparently thrived during the Late Cretaceous period. Struthiomimus skeletons have been found in many parts of the western United States and Canada, and in Asia as well.

Activity Safari

1. Ostriches can run at speeds up to forty-five miles per hour. Other top speeds for animals are listed below. Make a chart or graph on which you compare these speeds.

camel	10 miles per hour	lion	50 miles per hour
cheetah	70 miles per hour	roadrunner	25 miles per hour
giraffe	30 miles per hour	zebra	40 miles per hour

2. "Dinosaurize" your name! Write your name vertically in the middle of a piece of paper. Then add the names of prehistoric animals written horizontally so that they intersect with the letters of your name.

```
      S  T  R  U  T  H  I  O  M  I  M  U  S
                              T  I  T  A  N  O  S  A  U  R  U  S
            P  A  L  E  O  S  C  I  N  C  U  S
   E  U  O  P  L  O  C  E  P  H  A  L  U  S
                        P  I  N  A  C  O  S  A  U  R  U  S
            P  E  N  T  A  C  E  R  A  T  O  P  S
P  A  C  H  Y  C  E  P  H  A  L  O  S  A  U  R  U  S
```

Struthiomimus

Triceratops

Triceratops, the "three-horned face," lived in great numbers in the swamps and forests of western North America. This massive dinosaur was well protected from would-be predators. Its twenty-five-foot body was armed with three-foot horns, and its skull extended back to form a collar that shielded its neck. Triceratops had strong legs and a short, thick tail. Its great sharp beak was used to chop and chew the thick vegetation of its marshy habitat. This animal lived during the Late Cretaceous period and was one of the last dinosaurs to become extinct.

Activity Safari

1. All dinosaurs are extinct today. Hundreds of other animals are now threatened with extinction as a result of pollution, hunting, and habitat destruction. Make a poster encouraging the protection of one of these endangered animals.

bighorn sheep	gorilla
black rhinoceros	green turtle
blue whale	leopard
California condor	polar bear
giant anteater	Siberian tiger
giant panda	wolf

2. Use this pattern to make a Triceratops from stiff paper or tagboard. Fit the parts together as shown, and tape if necessary.

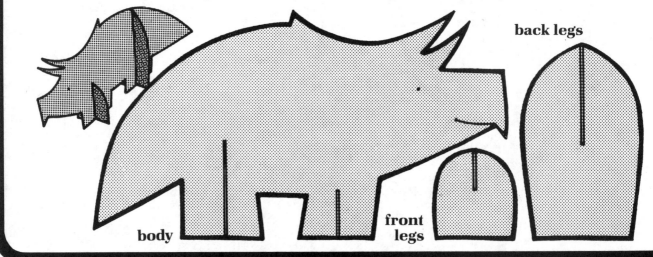

back legs

body

front legs

Triceratops

Tyrannosaurus

The "tyrant lizard" lived in northwestern North America during the Late Cretaceous period and was the greatest land carnivore of all time. Twenty feet tall and forty feet long, its seven-ton body was supported by massive legs that swung along in twelve-foot strides. This dinosaur's enormous body was well designed to defend and destroy. Its three-toed hind feet were armed with long talons. Its strange, small front legs had sharp claws. And dozens of seven-inch teeth lined its huge mouth. Anatosaurus frequently fell victim to this ravenous beast.

Activity Safari

1. How many steps would Tyrannosaurus take in walking from your classroom to the school cafeteria, or from your house to a neighbor's? With a partner and a twelve-foot piece of rope or string, pace off the distance and count the "Tyrannosaurusteps."

2. The head of an adult person would have come up to the knee of Tyrannosaurus. With these proportions in mind, draw a picture of yourself riding on or being chased by a tyrannosaur.

Tyrannosaurus

Dinosaur Facts

The head of Styracosaurus was protected by many horns and spines.

Pachycephalosaurus skulls were topped with a ten-inch-thick knob of bone.

Dilophosaurus had two thin, rounded crests on its head.

Sauromithoides had exceptionally large eyes and probably could see better than most other dinosaurs.

Barosaurus was a large, long-necked dinosaur. Its neck bones were each more than one yard long.

Torosaurus had a skull that was more than eight feet long.

Remains of Titanosaurus have been found in Asia, Europe, and South America.

Hypeselosaurus was a forty-foot-long dinosaur. A nest of its twelve-inch eggs was found in France.

The mouth of Psitticosaurus resembled a parrot's beak.

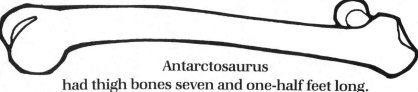

Antarctosaurus had thigh bones seven and one-half feet long.

Avimimus, or "bird mimic," had long legs, large eyes, and wings.

The nasal passages of Corythysaurus looped up through the crest on its head.

Saltopus was only about two feet long.

Halticosaurus was a hollow-boned animal with large holes in its skull.